Don't say that about MAINE!

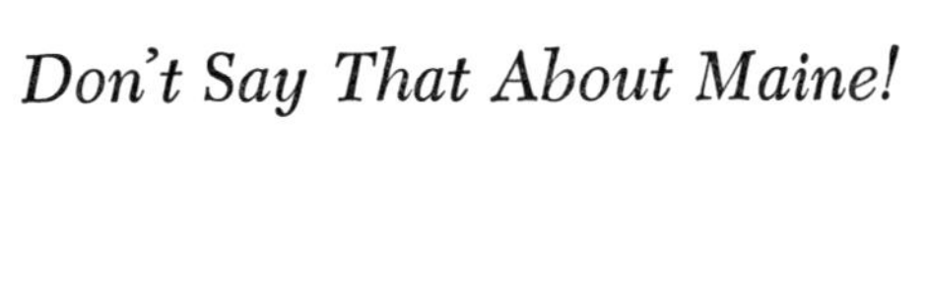
Don't Say That About Maine!

Don't say that about MAINE!

by
Kenneth Roberts

THE ANTHOENSEN PRESS
Portland, Maine 1986

Reprinted from the *Saturday Evening Post*

© 1948 The Curtis Publishing Company

ISBN 0–937703–00–1

The Anthoensen Press, Portland, Maine

"There may be an excess of cultivation as well as of
anything else, until civilization becomes pathetic. A
highly cultivated man—all whose bones can be bent!
Whose heaven-born virtues are but good manners! . . .
In civilization, as in a Southern latitude, man degen-
erates at length, and yields to the incursion of more
northern tribes."   Henry David Thoreau:
   A Week on the Concord and Merrimack Rivers.

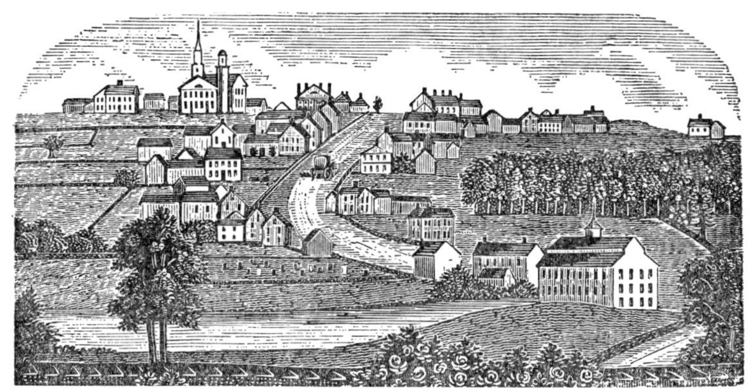

IN the course of the past few years I have had occasion to consult a considerable number of histories, diaries, journals and memoirs dealing with periods and events in which residents of New England—especially residents of my home state of Maine and my home town of Kennebunkport—took part. Those periods and events, I soon found, had been either glossed over or absurdly misrepresented by most of the historians who had undertaken to write about them—an inescapable state of affairs, since many historians who are acclaimed as historians are miserable historians, just as many supposedly great leaders are wretched leaders, many reputedly great architects are beneath contempt, and so on.

This discovery was neither new nor startling. Some of my fellow townsmen, in 1777, retreated from Fort Ticonderoga to Saratoga before the onrushing British army under Burgoyne. At Saratoga, the Americans made a stand, defeated the British twice, and captured all of them. During that interval between Ticonderoga and Saratoga, a young woman named Jennie McCrae was hideously murdered and mutilated by Burgoyne's Indians, and some of those Maine men must have been near by when it happened; so I tried to find out exactly how Jennie McCrae had met her end. A New York State historian had compiled all the accounts of Jennie McCrae's death—122 of them—and at the end had complained sadly that none of the 122 had agreed on anything except that Miss McCrae had been killed.

So many statements of supposed fact in the histories I consulted were so worthless that I eventually reached a point where, if I found a historian erring too grossly in judgment or facts, I discarded his entire book as being suspect.

Recently a great critical shouting arose over *A Study of History* by an English professor of history, Arnold J. Toynbee. It was, one American critic opined, the one book of the present century most assured of being read 100 years from now. Another critic declared that it was a veritable masterpiece of erudition—that Toynbee had more facts at his command and a wider vision than anyone else in the history of the world.

So I got the book; and since I am deeply interested in Maine and the experiences of her sons and daughters in the French and Indian War, the American Revolution, the wars with the Barbary States, the Mexican War, the War of 1812, the Civil War, as well as in more recent wars, I immediately looked in the index of Toynbee's effort to see whether Maine had been mentioned by this master of erudition.

To my pleasure, it had, but when I turned from the index to the text, my pleasure faded; for I found that Professor Toynbee must have had an off day when he marshaled his unrivaled assortment of facts on Maine and on New England.

The professor was struggling with an argument to the effect that the civilization of certain sections of this and other countries is high in the right sort of climate and low in the wrong sort of climate. The professor is not an easy writer, and frequently those who wish to understand him find themselves moving their lips and reverting to a preceding page to make sure that they really saw what they thought they saw.

If I understood the professor—and I did—he was arguing that big business, big men, important movements are restricted to areas that are chilly and rugged, but not too chilly nor too rugged. These areas, to make things easier for those who depend on Professor Toynbee to set them straight on civilization through the ages, the professor slangily calls areas of "optimum challenge"—meaning that the intellects, energies and business capacities of those permanently residing within those areas are so needled by the climate that they work while others sleep. They are full of stimulus, and they are constantly hustling, bustling and breeding judges, statesmen, authors, legal talent, architectural geniuses, artists, college professors, financiers and other serious-minded people who know how to get along in the world.

New England, says the professor, is such an area, and that is why New Englanders, in the early struggle for the control of the United States, outdistanced all their rivals.

But, the professor reminds his readers, in referring to "New England," he doesn't mean "all five of its little states." He means only three of them—Massachusetts, Connecticut and Rhode Island. The other two—New Hampshire and Maine—he assures us, are not important. They are really not New England at all. They're too cold. They have no optimum challenge, and the stimulus of those who dwell within them is thick and congealed.

The professor had either never been told that Vermont is

one of the New England states or the card on Vermont had inadvertently been dropped from his card-index system— a state of affairs that cannot fail to distress Vermonters who drowse through the pages of Toynbee's book during the next hundred years in the hope of learning about civilization, and whether or not they are civilized.

Since there is no Vermont in Toynbee's New England, Vermonters can never know with any degree of surety whether or not they are within the optimum-challenge belt; whether or not they have stimulus. They cannot whine to their fathers and mothers, begging them to move away from Vermont and into an optimum-challenge area like South Boston or Jersey City.

Massachusetts, Toynbee says, is all right. She's in the optimum-challenge belt and "has maintained her position in the intellectual sphere and to some extent in the industrial and commercial spheres as well." In this the professor is correct; some of the best Massachusetts people are not only aware of Vermont's existence but they send the fruits of their industry and commerce as far north as Burlington, Montpelier and Newport, Vermont, by way of the Boston & Maine and its subsidiary lines.

MAINE, however, Professor Toynbee tells his admiring and half-asleep readers, is so far out of the optimum-challenge belt as to be practically out of this world. Maine, Toynbee says, "has always been unimportant, and survives today as a kind of museum piece—a relic of seventeenth century New England inhabited by woodmen and water-men and hunters.

"These children of a hard country," Toynbee goes on, "now eke out their scanty livelihood by serving as 'guides' for pleasure seekers who come from the North American cities to spend their holidays in this Arcadian state, just because Maine is still what she was when many of these cities had not yet begun to arise out of the wilderness.

"Maine today," Toynbee concludes, "is at once one of the longest-settled regions of the American Union and one of the least urbanized and sophisticated."

In the last word of this casual dismissal of Maine, the professor has something, though he isn't conscious of it. Maine, as he says, is not sophisticated—nor does it wish to be. Complete definitions of the noun "sophistication" and of the verb "to sophisticate" are found in the *Century Dictionary and Cyclopedia.*

The transitive verb "sophisticate" has five meanings: (1) To clothe or obscure with fallacies; to falsify: (2) To overcome or delude by sophistry; to pervert; mislead: (3) To adulterate; render impure by admixture: (4) To deprive of simplicity; subject to the methods or influence of art: (5) To alter, either to deceive a reader or hearer, or to make a fancied improvement. The noun "sophistication" has substantially the same meanings.

A large part of the world, at the present time, is ruled or governed or influenced by true sophisticates: persons whose minds are foggy with fallacies; who exist for falsification; who are perverted and misled; who abhor simplicity and plunge headlong into fancied improvements, taxing and wasting the earnings of nonsophisticates at such a rate as to invite bankruptcy and ruin for all concerned.

Maine has always been impatient at such goings-on, as has her unknown—to Toynbee—sister state of Vermont, and both of them have frequently united politically against the hysterical and cockeyed sophistication of the other forty-six states. Neither Vermont nor Maine has any intention of letting itself be sophisticated, and although they may be— as Toynbee would surely have insisted had his all-encompassing vision been able to see Vermont—north of the optimum-challenge region, they can summon enough stimulus any day to keep out the sophisticates.

THE word "important" is a tricky one. In the last war it was applied to innumerable persons who intruded themselves into various military theaters of operation, at great expense to American taxpayers and for purposes of no value whatever to anyone. They were known to hard-working military, naval and aviation personnel as VIPS—Very Important People—and were loathed with an intensity impossible for the VIPS themselves to comprehend.

This meaning of "important" is recognized in Funk & Wagnall's *New Standard Dictionary of the English Language,* under Heading 2: "Of consequence in one's own estimation; pompous; pretentious."

Under this definition, Maine, as Toynbee says, has always been unimportant and highly allergic to importance. From what I've seen, there are fewer pompous and pretentious persons in Maine and Vermont than in any other states—which may be one of the reasons why American authors in greater and greater numbers are making their homes in Maine and adjacent states north of the optimum-challenge belt, doubtless to become woodmen, watermen and hunters, like Winslow Homer and other inhabitants of Maine.

Probably it's difficult for such a sophisticate as Toynbee to understand how the inhabitants of states like Maine and Vermont can deliberately court unimportance; how so many of them can be kind, generous, humorous, thoughtful, reserved, sensible, sociable, hard-working, independent, and bitterly intolerant of sham, waste, graft, loose thinking, loose living, bad government and historians who never heard of Vermont.

Calvin Coolidge, a gentleman born and reared far to the north of the area of optimum-challenge, paid tribute to his native state at a gathering held in Bennington, Vermont, on an anniversary of the Battle of Bennington, in which a group of Vermont woodmen, watermen and hunters annihilated a highly trained force of Hessians who were supporting an army from England's optimum-challenge area.

"Vermont," said unimportant Mr. Coolidge, "is the state I love. I could not look upon the peaks of Ascutney, Killington, Mansfield and Equinox without being moved in a way that no other scene could move me. It was here that I first saw the light of day; here I received my bride; here my dead lie pillowed on the loving breast of our everlasting hills. I love Vermont because of her hills and valleys, her scenery and invigorating climate, but most of all because of her indomitable people. They are a race of pioneers who have almost beggared themselves to serve others. If the spirit of liberty should vanish in other parts of our Union and support of our institutions should languish, it could all be replenished from the generous store held by the people of this brave little state of Vermont." But Vermont, according to Toynbee, doesn't exist.

LET us examine, for a moment, the State of Maine, that "sort of museum piece," that "relic of seventeenth century New England inhabited by woodmen and watermen and hunters."

There have been thirty-two Presidents of the United States. One, Franklin Pierce, was educated in the hard and unsophisticated atmosphere of Brunswick, Maine; and two, Chester Arthur and Calvin Coolidge, were natives of Vermont, so that the state Toynbee didn't know about, together with the state of woodmen, watermen and hunters, was responsible for better than one eleventh of our Presidents.

There have been thirteen Chief Justices of the United States Supreme Court. Maine provided one of them—Melville Fuller, who presided over the court for twenty-one years, from 1888 to 1910.

There have been forty-eight Speakers of the United States House of Representatives—a position at one time almost as influential as that of President. Two of those Speakers were

Maine men of outstanding ability—James G. Blaine and Thomas Brackett Reed.

Some of Maine's woodmen, watermen and hunters indulge in unexpected side lines or hobbies, and turn up in odd and out-of-the-way places as ship captains, newspaper owners and editors, teachers of Greek, English, history and all sorts of things in all sorts of colleges. They appear as bank presidents, book publishers, generals, doctors, opera singers, motion-picture directors, manufacturers, judges, railroad executives in a score of states—but at heart they remain woodmen, watermen and hunters still, just as Toynbee says.

Some of these woodmen, watermen and hunters actually go to school and occasionally read books. There is no perceptible difference between undergraduates and graduates of Colby College, Bates College and the University of Maine, and if they were mixed with an equal number of undergraduates from Cornell or Princeton, all of them wearing conventional academic gowns, not even a score of Toynbees could tell the woodmen, watermen and hunters from the sophisticates. Bowdoin College, which has had great teachers and great presidents, has graduated more celebrities per square inch of campus than any other American college. As Toynbee points out, nothing in Maine is important, but all her woodmen, watermen and hunter residents think highly of Bowdoin College and her woodmen-watermen graduates, Nathaniel Hawthorne, Henry Wadsworth Longfellow, Robert P. T. Coffin, Thomas Brackett Reed, Admiral Robert Peary, Donald MacMillan, President Franklin Pierce, Chief Justice Melville Fuller, Supreme Court Justice Harold Burton and innumerable others, including the present president of Bowdoin, whose hardy woodman-waterman-hunting training somehow gets him out of the seventeenth century and permits him to be a trustee of the Carnegie Foundation, of Athens College in Greece, of Wellesley College, and a member of the United States Naval Academy's visiting committee. It was the wife of a Bowdoin professor who squared away at her desk in Brunswick and wrote some unimportant chapters destined to be read by millions. The *Encyclopædia Britannica* refers to them as "a factor which must be reckoned in summing up the moving causes of the Civil War." The chapters became *Uncle Tom's Cabin*, and the lady was Harriet Beecher Stowe.

Incidentally, Senator Austin, of the Little State That Isn't There, heads the United States delegation to the United Nations, is a staunch supporter of the European Recovery Program—which is interesting if not important to a good many million Europeans who will never hear of Toynbee. At the same time, the woodmen, watermen and hunters of a single county—Aroostook—in the Museum-Piece State help Europeans to recover by sending 6,000,000 bushels of potatoes to Europe during the winter.

I HAD some communication, recently, with two children of this hard country who, according to Toynbee, "now eke out [a] scanty livelihood by serving as 'guides' for plea-sure seekers." John R. Newell does his eking at the Bath Iron Works Corporation, of Bath, Maine, and Admiral John H. Brown, Jr., does his guiding while acting as commandant of the Portsmouth Navy Yard at Kittery, Maine.

Both Mr. Newell and Admiral Brown seemed to think that Toynbee had been accepting information from sophisti-cates who sit on the floor and talk about things they don't understand—two pastimes that are viewed with a jaundiced eye in Maine.

England, prior to the past war, in spite of lying in Toyn-bee's area of optimum-challenge, and being excessively ur-banized and sophisticated, had diminished profoundly in human response. Her statesmanship had sunk so low, in fact, that some Englishmen openly admitted that England's so-called statesmen were behaving as though brought up in Greenland, which Toynbee classes as a land of pessimum challenge.

As a result of this, England several times found herself on

the verge of becoming a German province, for she lacked the destroyers and the submarines to protect her supply ships from German attack. Fortunately for England, Maine's woodmen, watermen and hunters had knocked off from their wood cutting, canoeing and hunting long enough to build, at the Bath Iron Works, thirty destroyers prior to and during the First World War. Seven of these went to England in the fifty-destroyer deal that gave England her first breathing spell. Between 1934 and "Pearl Harbor," the woodmen, watermen and hunters had gone to work again and constructed fifteen destroyers at the Bath Iron Works. After "Pearl Harbor," the Bath Iron Works took on an additional 40,000 woodmen, watermen and hunters to build and deliver eighty of the Navy's largest destroyers, two hundred and forty-four Liberty ships and thirty British ocean-class ships. At Kittery, meanwhile, another group were turning out American submarines and, even before the United States entered the war, repairing English submarines—*Pandora*, *Parthian* and *Truant*, all of them so badly bunged about that they practically had to be rebuilt.

MAINE has suffered considerably from the warped judgments of more urbanized and sophisticated people from sections which Toynbee believes to be fuller of stimulus. For example, Edward Preble, a Maine waterman for whom streets, squares and hotels have been named in various parts of his native state, was, to my way of thinking, one of the great captains of all time. At the period when he was eking out a scant living by guiding the United States Frigate *Constitution,* Maine was full of mariners—sea captains—just like him, though the diminutive size of the American Navy prevented their abilities from being recognized in Navy records.

When the Tripolitan Navy, under a renegade Scot admiral, began to throw its weight around, American squadrons were sent to the Mediterranean to put a quietus on his activities. Unfortunately, the first three American commodores to command the American ships were from areas of optimum challenge, were hopelessly incompetent and got exactly nowhere.

Then Preble was sent out in the *Constitution* to take charge. His dramatic and daring attacks on Tripoli won him

world-wide fame, and led the Pope to write, "Commodore
Preble, with a small force and in a short space of time, has
done more for the cause of Christianity than the most power-
ful nations of Christendom have done for ages."

But Preble was unfortunate: in the American Navy at that
time there were more important commodores from more sophisticated and urban centers. Consequently, just after
Preble's two gallant attacks had almost blown the Bashaw of
Tripoli backward into the middle of the seventeenth century, a higher-ranking commodore arrived in the Mediterranean, hailing from an area of optimum challenge. Thus
Preble was automatically superseded, and, as a result—
since his superseder was incompetent, dilatory, stupid, and
sick to boot—everything that Preble had accomplished was
nullified.

THAT indomitable quality of which Mr. Coolidge spoke when referring to the people of Vermont is peculiarly apparent to any person who has an understanding mind and eyes to see. This indomitable quality was strikingly apparent during the Civil War, when Maine furnished the Union Army and Navy with more men, proportionately, than did any other state.

I shall be specific about the commander of one of those Maine regiments, because he seems to me to be a concentrate of the unsophisticated qualities that Toynbee finds so regrettable and so revolting. These qualities have always existed throughout this "relic of seventeenth century New England inhabited by woodmen, watermen and hunters." These qualities—as apparent today as they were in 1863— are integrity, modesty, diligence, thrift, kindness, coolness, cultivation and endurance.

Joshua Lawrence Chamberlain was born and brought up in Brewer, Maine, a town so far north of the optimum-challenge belt that stimulus is practically nonexistent in it—if Toynbee is to be believed—except occasionally, during an August drought. Living, as he did, in a shipbuilding community, the little Chamberlain boy's complete lack of sophistication caused him to make a point of climbing to the main truck of every vessel launched and hanging his hat on it—something that no sophisticate would be caught dead doing.

While still a schoolboy, he was a farmer, a navigator, an expert marksman and an omnivorous reader, in addition to working in a brickyard, a ropewalk, and ardently devouring all the poetry on which he could lay his hands.

A long-standing peculiarity of Maine is the addiction of great numbers of its woodmen-watermen-hunters to the reading and writing of poetry. As far back as 1888 an 850-page book of poems by 400 Maine poets was published, and fifty years later the Poetry Fellowship of Maine was encouraging such watermen, woodmen and hunters as were eager to follow in the footsteps of those other watermen, woodmen and hunters, Henry Wadsworth Longfellow, Edwin Arlington Robinson, Edna St. Vincent Millay and Robert P. Tristram Coffin.

Before he finished school, Chamberlain was obsessed to become a missionary, but to be a missionary he had to become a clergyman, and to be a clergyman he had to go to college, and to go to college he had to know Greek. So he retreated to the attic every day for six months and memorized Kühner's unabridged Greek grammar from alpha to omega. This gained him admission to Bowdoin, where he took honors in every course.

During his vacations he eked out his scanty livelihood by teaching sailors and millmen, and when he graduated in 1852 he entered the Bangor Theological Seminary, studied Hebrew, Syriac and Arabic, read theology in Latin and church history in German. At the same time he taught the German language and literature to "choice classes" of young ladies, as well as serving as supervisor of schools in Brewer.

Unworried by his lack of sophistication, Chamberlain took his master's degree in 1855, was immediately made an instructor in religion, and a year later was elected professor of rhetoric and oratory. In 1857 he took on the added labors of instructor of French and German, and in 1861 was elected professor of the modern languages of Europe. Just as he was about to leave for Europe to study, the Union Army encountered a series of serious reverses, and Chamberlain, instead of dodging the army or hunting a secluded nook in Washington, as more sophisticated souls might have done, decided that the Union Army was more in need of his services than was Bowdoin College. When he announced his intention of going to the front, he was offered a colonelcy in a newly formed Maine regiment, but refused it on the ground that he didn't know enough about soldiering—a dreadful revelation of the awful degeneration of men's minds when they live in a sort of museum piece, far removed from areas of optimum challenge.

On the eighth of August, 1862, Chamberlain was made lieutenant colonel of the 20th Maine, and in four weeks' time his regiment was in the front line at Bull Run. Four months later, these woodmen, watermen and hunters had been through the battles of Antietam and Fredericksburg, which may have been forgotten by the all-seeing Toynbee, but were long remembered by thousands of widows in that unimportant relic of the seventeenth century, the state of Maine.

It was at Gettysburg, on July 2, 1863, that Chamberlain really caused raised eyebrows among those from optimum-challenge areas, received the Congressional Medal of Honor for "conspicuous personal gallantry and distinguished service," and was actually recommended by his superiors for promotion to the rank of brigadier general. Unfortunately, he was without political backing among the sophisticates, and as has usually been the case in all American armies under such circumstances, the recommendations were pigeonholed in the War Department.

It's difficult—for Toynbee—to understand how a man from such a hard country as Maine could have done what Chamberlain did in spite of lacking stimulus. Let others than Toynbee tell about those unsophisticated and unurbanized antiques from Maine. Gen. James Rice, commanding the 1st Division, 1st Corps, Army of the Potomac, wrote of Chamberlain: "He held the extreme left of the entire Union line, and for the brilliant success of the conflict upon the second day of the battle, history will give credit to the bravery and unflinching fortitude of the 20th Maine Volunteers under his command, more than to any equal number of men upon the field. This conduct has rendered the honor of his State in arms imperishable."

Col. W. H. Powell, USA, wrote: "Historians have exhausted themselves in describing the actions of the 'Peach Orchard,' and the events of the third day at Gettysburg. Great stress has been laid upon the results of Pickett's charge, while famous pictures have presented that scene to the gaze of the American public; but the truth of history is that the little brigade of Vincent's, with the self-sacrificing valor of the 20th Maine, under the gallant leadership of Joshua L. Chamberlain, fighting amidst the scrub oak and rocks in that vale between the Round Tops on the 2nd of July, 1863, saved to the Union arms the historic field of Gettysburg. Had they faltered for one instant—had they not exceeded their actual duty—while the left of the 3rd Corps was swung in the air half a mile to the right and front off Little Round Top, there would have been no grand charge of Pickett, and Gettysburg would have been the mausoleum of departed hopes for the national cause; for Longstreet would have enveloped Little Round Top, captured all on its crest from the rear, and held the key of the whole position."

Chamberlain was just as unsophisticated in the Battle of Petersburg, when he stormed Rives' Salient on June 18, 1864. He had a splendid brigade of five veteran regiments, and a fine new regiment of 1,000 men. With this, earlier in the day, he had carried an advanced position named "Fort Hell." He brought up three batteries to hold it, but soon received an oral order, through a more sophisticated staff officer from an optimum-challenge area, to charge the enemy's main works, some two or three hundred yards in front. This was one of their strongest entrenched positions, and Chamberlain—after the manner of unsophisticates from Maine—doubted the authenticity of the order, as his brigade was a mile away from the main army, out of sight of his superior commanders, and without support on either flank, while the point to be carried was held by double his numbers behind entrenchments with twenty pieces of artillery to give a direct and cross fire at canister range. To complicate matters, a fort enfiladed the ground over which he must approach.

When Chamberlain questioned his orders, he was told he must attack alone, so that the rest of the army could "guide" on him. Knowing that he was an unimportant man from an unimportant state, and so without stimulus, he sent his men forward in two waves and led them himself into a terrible cross fire. His horse was killed instantly. When his standard-bearer was shot, Chamberlain picked up the flag and went on. Why not? He was unsophisticated. When a marsh stopped him, he obliqued his men around it and was shot through both hips. With typical Maine unsophistication, he propped himself on his saber and continued to direct the attack. Loss of blood brought him flat on the ground, but he still continued to give the orders that prevented his men from being taken in flank and completely wiped out.

After the battle, he was given up by regular army surgeons, and his death announced throughout the North, but his life was saved by his brother, Thomas, then major of the 20th Maine, who brought up the surgeon of that regiment, Doctor Shaw, who was so unsophisticated that he worked and watched over him with tireless fidelity and skill from midnight to dawn. Being in the extreme advance of the army, there were no means at hand for his proper care. Barely alive from loss of blood, he was borne sixteen miles on men's shoulders on a scorching midsummer day; then sent by transport to Annapolis Naval School Hospital. Here he lay in a tent in agony for two months, his surgeons daily expecting his death. But he was an unsophisticate from an unurbanized community, so, miraculously, he recovered and asked to be returned to duty in the field. He received the remarkable compliment of being applied for by General Ayres to command the regulars consolidated into a brigade in his division.

When Chamberlain commanded the Union troops to whom Lee surrendered, he received the surrendering army with a salute of honor. If he'd had the least trace of sophistication, he would doubtless have bombarded it with lemon pies.

After he had been elected governor of Maine by the largest majority ever given in that state, he stepped hard on the toes of those advanced thinkers who were advocating prohibition and denouncing capital punishment. He refused to establish a state constabulary to enforce prohibition by search and seizure, and he insisted on the execution of a Negro who had been convicted of a series of atrocious crimes. The prohibitionists and the sentimentalists set out to raise a tide of popular feeling against such unsophisticated and backward behavior, but Maine, with seventeenth-century perversity, persisted in supporting Chamberlain's unsophistication. Bowdoin College, having always had a bucolic and unurbanized leaning toward unsophistication, made him her president in 1871. There's no dodging the fact that unsophistication goes big in Maine.

A great newspaperman, reviewing Civil War leaders and battles, wrote: "The brush of artist never had a grander theme than Chamberlain at Petersburg. It should be put on canvas or sculptured in marble and placed in the rotunda of the capitol at Washington to show to the world the stuff of which American patriots are made. As an example to inspire patriotism it would rank with Leonidas and his three hundred Spartans."

ISN'T there something wrong here?

CONFIDENTIALLY, no! And neither Toynbee nor any other historian can make me accept Maine as a Vacationland or as a kind of museum piece, a relic of seventeenth-century New England inhabited by woodmen, watermen, hunters who eke out their scanty livelihood by serving as guides.

As I said in the beginning, I have learned to discard the writings of any historian who errs too grossly. Toynbee's utterances about Maine are so ludicrous that I doubt everything that Toynbee has ever written. If he's so wrong about Maine, he's probably equally wrong about the Primitive Muslim Arabs, the conquests of the Euthydemic Bactrian Greek princes, the creative rôle of Russia in the Great Society, and all the other subjects about which he writes so glibly and so dully. I wouldn't trust him to write correctly about anything.

As far as Maine is concerned, Toynbee's *Study of History* goes to the attic to join Parson Weems' *Life of George Washington*.

Don't Say That About Maine was composed in Linotype Caledonia, a sturdy, New England typeface designed by W. A. Dwiggins. This edition consists of 1,500 copies which were printed letterpress at the Anthoensen Press, Portland, Maine.